Atlantic

Atlantic

Selected Poems of Faith

Kenneth Steven

with photography by Kristina Hayward

CASCADE *Books* · Eugene, Oregon

ATLANTIC
Selected Poems of Faith

Cascade Books
An Imprint of Wipf and Stock Publishers
199 W. 8th Ave., Suite 3
Eugene, OR 97401

www.wipfandstock.com

PAPERBACK ISBN: 979-8-3852-3810-1
HARDCOVER ISBN: 979-8-3852-3811-8
EBOOK ISBN: 979-8-3852-3812-5

Cataloguing-in-Publication data:

Names: Steven, Kenneth [author]. | Hayward, Kristina [photographer]

Title: Atlantic : selected poems of faith / by Kenneth Steven ; with photographs
by Kristina Hayward.

Description: Eugene, OR: Cascade Books, 2025

Identifiers: ISBN 979-8-3852-3810-1 (paperback) | ISBN 979-8-3852-3811-8
(hardcover) | ISBN 979-8-3852-3812-5 (ebook)

Subjects: LCSH: Poetry. | Nature in poetry. | Poetry—Religious. | English po-
etry—Scottish authors. | Christian poetry—English.

Classification: PS3569 S74 2025 (print) | PS3569 (ebook)

VERSION NUMBER 06/12/25

For Mother Seraphima and all the Sisters of Holy Nativity
Convent with love and grateful thanks for your friendship

Contents

Acknowledgements

The author wishes to acknowledge permission for the re-publication of the following poems.

From my books *Iona* (2000), *Salt and Light* (2007), *Out of the Ordinary* (2020), and *Seeing the Light* (2023): "That Year," "Skellig Michael," "Together," "Autumn," "The Holy Isle," "Kyrie," "The Birth," "Serpentine," "Of Price and Worth" and "Gift." Reprinted with the kind permission of Hymns Ancient and Modern.

From my collection *West* (2019): "Journey" and "Salt." Reprinted with the kind permission of Wild Goose Publications.

The following poems originally appeared in my book *Island* (Saint Andrew, 2009): "The Birth of the Foal," "Columba," "Clonmacnoise," "The Stars," "The Illuminated Manuscript," "Balranald," "A Poem for Ann," "Iona," "Argyll," "Prayer," "Sometimes," "The Strangest Gift," "Daffodils," "Kilmelford," "Serpentine," "Gift," "The Small Giant," "The Well," "Island," "September," "The Beehive Cells," "Awakening," "Hebrides," "Remember," "Mushrooms," "The Death of Columba," "The Heron," "Winter Light," and "Remembering the Amish." Rights have reverted to the author.

The following poems originally appeared in my collections *Evensong* (SPCK, 2011) and *Coracle* (SPCK, 2014): "Coracle," "Solace," "Enough," "The Summer House," "Iona," "Gliese 581," "Evensong," "Pears," "The Fishing," and "The Hermit's Cell." Rights have reverted to the author.

Introduction

I grew up in the middle of Scotland, in the beautiful heartland of Perthshire filled with mighty rivers and many hills, long lochs and great moorlands. In short, there's much wildscape, as I like to think of it. Not many towns and few major roads, somewhere it's easy to walk into the hills and find silence. I was fortunate in having parents who were passionate about wild places; from a young age I was taken into the outdoors and taught about wildscape. I learned about birdsong, about the stories behind all manner of places, and often had the privilege of meeting the people who lived on the edge of that wildscape. My mother's family were from the Highlands proper, many of them Gaelic-speaking, and the experience of that world filtered into my writing early on. There were poems about the birth of lambs and about collecting horse chestnuts, about seeing otters and walking deep in the hills—because I was experiencing these things.

But Perthshire, at the heart of inland Scotland, lacked one thing: the sea. For all the autumn, winter, and spring months, I missed the sea terribly, was aware of being landlocked. I missed the one element I couldn't have of the wild world and counted the days until summer returned and we could head west to the Atlantic.

For each year without fail we'd visit one or other of the islands off the Scottish west coast, in the Hebrides. I began getting to know them from a young age and sensed the uniqueness of each one early on. Sometimes the differences between them were hard to define; it was as simple as a feeling, a feeling that might almost be described as a slightly different colour. But what I know for sure is that at the very centre of all those west coast islands was Iona.

This little pebble of an island is all but three miles long and not more than one and a half wide. I felt the difference of it just as my mother had done many years before when she first visited Iona. Even yet I find it impossible to define; I love all the islands of the Atlantic west, yet I will know always that the jewel at their heart is Iona.

It has been described as one of the thin places of the world, somewhere the veil between this existence and that of the spiritual realm is somehow more liable to tear. Where they *meet*—sometimes, or more often—for many. Not everyone experiences the thinness of that veil on Iona; some keep coming here year on year and love the translucent blue-green seas and the golden sands of the beaches, but it doesn't go much beyond that. I go back and back to define more deeply all the time what I've experienced here, I know, since I was five years old.

It's impossible to know just how old that "thinness" is. St Columba landed on Iona from Ireland in 563 AD, but it's all but certain he came here after the arrival of the Druids, that they had been present here however long before. But why had the Druids been drawn to Iona? By that point we can't dig any deeper into history; we can have all the ideas and beliefs we like, but none of them can be proved. A year or so ago at a book festival I had a conversation with a fellow wirter who spoke about a path marking the way to Iona that dates from the Stone Age. All I know is that this "thinness" feels truly ancient; it doesn't feel something laid here by our human presence, though perhaps the long centuries of prayer may have deepened it. Somehow those roots feel as deep as Iona.

But to build on what we do know: Columba, as I've stated, came here with his twelve followers from Ireland in 563 AD. Here he founded his monastery, on the east side of the island facing the neighbouring island of Mull. And from here the monks went out as missionaries with the Christian gospel; they travelled to England and they went deep into Europe. Whenever possible they travelled by boat. We live our modern lives by roads; the sea and inland lakes were their highways and they were skilled navigators. They were built of stern stuff; there's sometimes a dangerous tendency to render them too gentle and soft. I like to think of those early Celtic Christian monks as being warriors on the outside yet possessing a passionate intensity, fierce love. We can perceive that from the stories they created, not least in relation to their honouring of the natural world. The story that for me says most about that love of God's creation is St Kevin and the Blackbird. Of course it's not strictly true in terms of the narrative, but it's most certainly true in terms of that devotion it shows the Celtic Christians displaying for all things that lived. For everything was created by a loving God.

Some of the monks didn't want the green ease of Iona, they wanted instead to find the wildest and most austere rocks in the western islands where there were no temptations and where they could hear more easily the voice of the divine. It was about gaining a kind of martydom. That couldn't be understood any longer by being eaten by a lion or being put to the sword; by and large Christianity had been accepted without conflict. Martyrdom had to be understood in new ways: the sea became the desert and setting out into the unknown ocean in faith an act of martyrdom. The greater the privations they experienced the greater that martyrdom. Some went out from Iona (as they did from Ireland) in tiny vessels and remained in these rocky islets where they had nothing but fresh water; it's my belief they would have remained there for forty days and forty nights before returning to Iona and the mother church to be restored for however long.

Some were explorer monks; they voyaged north and further north in open boats until they reached Iceland and Faroe and even Greenland. They'd have travelled during the summer months and at night they would have steered by the stars.

St Columba became well known in his own lifetime; others were curious and came to find Iona. It became the shining light at the heart of the Celtic Christian world. It was no quiet place of gentle retreat; instead it was somewhere loud with the excited chatter of voices arguing about all manner of learned things, by no means only religious beliefs. To all intents and purposes it was an early university.

After the death of St Columba he became even better known because a biography was written of his life. That drew others to Iona, and many now chose to be buried here because it had been Columba's island, a place of holiness. Many kings were brought to be laid to rest in the shadow of his monastery, both Scots and Norwegian. A hundred years after that the greatest treasure of the Celts was created on Iona: the Book of Kells. It was only taken to Ireland for safe-keeping for fear it might be snatched by the marauding Vikings, who had pillaged Iona before and knew that here rich pickings were to be found.

All of this story has been written through my life and my writing, and I know I'm still learning about the island and its journey, and about the literal place. One of the great joys in recent years has been the leading of Celtic Christian retreats on Iona with Kristina my wife. It feels somehow as though the right people have found their way here. It's been special too creating a podcast each month inspired by the Celtic Christian story of Iona, to weave that through poetry and prose. It's only a few years since good friends found ancient oak trees in a corner of the island, oaks that may go right back to the time of Columba and his followers. I still have to find them, as I still have to find many other places on this tiny island that is somehow far bigger than ever it will look on any map.

The Birth of the Foal

My eyes still fought with sleep. Out over the fields
mist lay in grey folds, from vague somewheres
curlews rose up with thin trails of crying. Our lanterns
rocked in soft globes of yellow, our feet
slushed through the early morning thickness of the grass.

She lay on her side, exhausted by her long night;
the hot smells of flanks and head and breath
ghosted from her spread length.
Sunlight cracked from the broken yolk of the skies,
ruptured the hills, spangled our eyes and blinded us
flooded the pale glows of our lanterns.

There he lay in a pool of his own wetness:
four long spindles scrabbling, the bigness of his head, a bag of a body—
all struggling to find one another, to join up, to glue
into the single flow of a birthright. He fought
for the first air of his life, noised like a child.

His mother, still ran and torn from the scar of his birth,
turned, and her eyes held him,
the great harsh softness of her tongue stilled his struggle.

We knelt in the wet grass, dumbed
by a miracle, by something bigger than the sun.

Kyrie

When the beautiful world spread her branches
over and above your head
the sun curled the edges of your smile,
brought drops of shining when the moonlight fell
across the wide open land of your hands.

How tender the tomorrows in your gentle feet;
how fragile their miles that must not lose
nor fail the nakedness of touch, of breath—
mending the web's thread, healing her skin.

In time you will put your life before the canon
and your hand where the trees are cut,
pouring long selfless love back for the wound
that bled you, opened out your world
when first your feet stood made below the stars.

Columba

A film lies across the water meadows
like a muslin shawl. Birds lament
among rushes, their low voices trailing
like beads of glass. The sun has not been born yet,
remains under woods and hills.
Columba goes down, his ankles buried by soft water,
by green fronds, slippery, making no more sound
than a deer. The swans drift over the water,
so white they hurt the eyes. He stops,
forgetting everything as he watches the stoop and silver
of their grace, the sudden rippling of their backs
cast by wind, the furling of the huge wings
like shards of ice. They too are prayers, personified,
awakenings of God in the morning water land.
He goes on, to the strange stone head
carved and lying dormant in the grass;
those wide eyes that never blinked,
the ringlets of stone hair curling
about the enigma of a half-buried face.
He comes here, even though the smiths who cut this
have known only gods of wood and loam,
have chanted under the wheels of stars,
made strange offerings of wheat and fire and gold.
Here at the water meadow's end he finds the Christ
ripe in his heart, his lips brim with words

that soar like larks into the sky,
almost as if some spring of light and joy
wells from the ground beneath.
He kneels in the wet softness of the earth
and smells the springtime yellow in his veins—
becomes the place he prays in.

Coracle

A round of dryness, one man strong
woven and stitched to bob
the slow fishponds and the deeper creeks,
the waterways of crannogs:

out even to the up and down of sea,
the blue bell of water that does not end,
but reaches, by the compass of the stars,
another island and a new beginning.

Clonmacnoise

Wrapped in the wool of winter;
the fields breathed with frost—

even the Shannon confused,
searching in ribbons through the fields,

the sun straining to see
like a single frozen eye—

we came to Clonmacnoise
fifteen hundred years too late

crows in the ivied silence of round towers,
gravestones bent as though in penitence;

chapels fallen in upon themselves
like broken faith.

And yet I could imagine
in the once upon a time of Ireland

men awakening to break the wells
to bring in steamings of white water;

keeping the turf fire's glow,
storm after December storm

here where they had caught God's light
(so fragile, yet alive for ever)

to bear it bright
out into the dark places of the earth.

The Stars

From the age of five my sight was smudged as a mole's;
I wore tortoiseshell-rimmed glasses that were never quite clean
and the stars looked white and indistinct,
vague pearls in a distant heaven.
On my fifteenth birthday my parents gave me lenses—
little cupped things that drifted into sight across my irises.
Driving home with them that night I suddenly caught sight of something,
got out by the edge of the field and looked,
amazed and disbelieving as if Christ himself had healed my eyes,
for the stars were crackling and sparking
like new-cut diamonds on the velvet of a jeweller's window,
so near and clear I could have stretched and held them,
carried them home in my own pocket.
That was the gift my parents gave me on my birthday—
the stars.

The Illuminated Manuscript

They brought me here from Ireland, still a boy
to begin their book.

I remember the day I left—
soft bread, a silvering of geese, the sound of my mother.

Now I slip the stone of these steps every day
long before dawn, breathe the dark

and hear the whelming of the winds about this fastness
before my one candle like a petal of gorse

flutters the shadows in ghosts over the cold walls.
Out of the thin window I watch the sea all winter

heave and drag like a dying man,
the skies blackened and bruised.

Some days there is nothing in the pen except
my own emptiness; I hold it hoping

until the stars blow out from the attic of the skies
and a ledge of moon lifts across the hills.

Just sometimes something breaks inside
like the brittle lid of a casket

and pours out light onto the waiting page.

Balranald

This place on the edge of living
shut in by the gales and the whipped water
broken like sweet cream on the toothless rocks.
Here the birds shuffle along the sand on tiptoe,
rise with weeping into a mouth of wind
and the gulls scream like Viking raiders.
There, out on the last of the eye's journey,
sun coins a golden headland, the sky lights blue,
and suddenly the day is made of summer.
Who can translate the curlew's sadness
into late evening across the moor—
a voice as precious as psalms.

Journey

I have gone into a landscape
not to come back different
but more myself. It can take days
to go into the hills and listen.

Everything is miles of silence:
a stretch of loch so blue it can't be real,
an eagle floating in the sky,
at night the skies a breath of stars.

I leave behind my loudness
for a time; remember what it means
to swim again, to feel
way out of my depth.

A Poem for Ivars

A picture of Latvia:
you as a boy lifting potatoes behind a horse,
swallows ticking wings in a farmyard sky,
the generals of winter a day yet closer.

In the hungry faces, the simple hands,
and this hard road through the furrows of Moscow,
I see richer earth still living, wooden songs
that could pull your people's faith.

If a man should come now to your door
selling motorways, a rustle of money in his eyes;
do not buy his road, for it leads
to all our lost riches, our need of God.

Iona

Is this place really nearer to God?
Is the wall thin between our whispers
and his listening? I only know
the world grows less and less—
here what matters is conquering the wind,
coming home dryshod, getting the fire lit.
I am not sure whether there is no time here
or more time; whether the light is stronger
or just easier to see. That is why
I keep returning, thirsty, to this place
that is older than my understanding,
younger than my broken spirit.

That Year

The plough hit a hollowness,
a missing thing whose sound stopped him,
brought him to his knees,
his both hands dragging that wet blackness back.

A hole in the earth. Seven, and the last light
honeyed from the west across the fields.
He heard his heart; lowered himself through the emptiness,
dropped into the softness of a cave kept silent
who knew how many hundred years.

His eyes saw only darkness, then slowly woke, found walls
curving the place to a beehive, a cupped heart
woven out of careful stone, shaped smooth to something
whose name was buried with the hands that built it.

Yet all at once he knew what this had been;
the whispers, soft as candle flames, breathed his hearing,
a peace shone from the dark and welled his heart
so full he dragged the tangle of his hat away, stood bowed,
as somewhere up above the curlews sang their evensong.

Argyll

All down the coast
the air was full of fish and sunset.

By nine the lemon-coloured cottages
were warm windows glowing over the bays.

Far west the light a rim of blue and white,
Jura and Mull and Scarba all carved from shining.

On the way home we stopped to listen to the dark,
to the sea coming huge over a hundred beaches.

In among the trees, in windless stillness,
the bats were flitting, weaving patterns with the air.

That night I did not want the stars to rise at all;
I wanted it to be like this and nothing more

looking west into the sunset
to the very end of the world.

Prayer

If you do not believe in God
go on a blue spring day across these fields:
listen to the orchids, race the sea, scent the wind.

Come back and tell me it was all an accident,
a collision of blind chance
in the empty hugeness of space.

Skellig Michael

Remember when they brought you here
in a bob of boat that lurched and swung
beneath this barren whaleback in the sea.
Then you started climbing rock by rock;
tugged and tousled by the wind each step
until at last you stood on top,
held in the breathlessness of blown blue sky—
the whole gusting wildness of this world
out in the pounding of the seas.

Then the building began;
the heaving up of boulder after boulder,
balancing them together till you'd made
a beehive you could creep inside.
Dry, dark and deep: a cave of peace,
a cocoon where three of you could sleep
after the long prayers of the place
they called the sanctuary.

Just sometimes you came out bleary-eyed
to stand at midnight in the silence
of a night left silver, stars
like mist across the skies, that stillness
reaching to the edges of the sea.
You knew for sure that something greater than all this
had made it beautiful, had breathed it into being.

Island

In
all
the
rush
and
hurry
of
our
lives
we
need
so
much
just
now
and
then
to
find
an
island

The Strangest Gift

Sister Mary Teresa gave me a wasps' nest from the convent garden—
just the startings, the first leaves, a cocoon of whisperings—
made out of thousands of buzzings.
To think that these yellow-black thugs
could make such finery, such parchment,
a whole home telling the story of their days,
written and wrought so perfect
stung me, remembering how I'd thumped them
with thick books, reduced them to squashes on walls,
nothing more than broken bits on carpets.
This little bowl, this bit of beginning,
rooted out by the gardener, reminds me
of something bigger I keep choosing to forget,
about what beauty is, and where that beauty's found.

Solace

I look back through my mind and see
the days when forest wolved the land in mystery
and light was cradled out of coracles
in wild and wintered island storm.

All night and every night the rip and snarl of wind,
and this their task alone, to guard the light they had been given—
the flutter of that single flame
keeping out the whole world of the dark.

Daffodils

They flurry over the first raw green of the hills,
trumpet the Easter fields;
bright flags with their orange yolks
bending under the flaying cruelty of April winds.

As if to prove that Calvin got it wrong,
that dark-lipped Luther in the cold austerity of history
threw away the warm laughter of love
for the bare bones of theology.

The Birth

He is born, she whispered,
go down and look at him.
Six in the morning and I said nothing,
still woolly with dreams,
buried in the room's warm darkness.
I struggled slowly into clothes,
thudded down the wooden staircase.
Outside it was March, the land all scabbed and sore
with winter; the wind a rusty blade
cutting the eyebrows and the wrists,
the river whiskying away downstream and roaring
with snow and stories.
At the barn I opened a door into darkness,
blinked in the thick, warm smell of hay.
A bit of wet sunlight broke through the window;
I saw the mother like a granite boulder—
even her eyes exhausted—
that thin patch of lamb beside her,
shivering. He tried to push up the sky from above him,
and his legs melted away like wax;
he cried a single time.
I went closer, on soft and reverent feet,
and this was suddenly a Bethlehem,
his voice a child's, as vulnerable as Christ's.

Of Price and Worth

Let the ordinary be in your hand;
hold it open and imagine a bird landing,
offering all it possesses in trust
to come to you.

Learn to look for the little things
that weigh nothing at all,
but fill the heart with such light
they can never be measured.

Kilmelford

A bit of country soft with rain
smelling green, ringing like glass
with the songs of warblers and wrens.

Through thigh-deep wheat fields
Columba's chapels like still in prayer,
fallen in on themselves with age.

Now at nightfall the boats sleep
with the white glows of their lamps
leaning out over August lochs.

The stars flow into the water of the skies
like pearls from a broken necklace
and the light is long, the night is huge.

Columba's Isle

And God said:
Let there be a place made of stone
out off the west of the world,
roughed nine months by gale,
rattled in Atlantic swell.

A place that rouses each Easter
with soft blessings of flowers
and shocks of white shell sand;
a place found only sometimes
by those who have lost their way.

The Summer House

There is the hush of sea in an open window
and a child coming running under bare sunlight
with news of shells and a big whale.

There is more time: life slows to a single heartbeat,
the days flow into endless places, stretch like shadows.

The world we carry does not weigh so much,
but seems to fall as simple as a starfish
in something we can see is beautiful again.

Sometimes we ride the sea, go out to climb the waves,
to have the laughter knocked from us in play
and come back breathless to a barefoot house
to listen, listen to the late day made of curlews.

A huge moon rolls into the sky, ghost-white,
lighting every field, and breeze silks the hills.

All night we dream of nothing
like children who have never learned of sin.

Serpentine

A little cave of green stone
smoothed by centuries of sea
to a pebble smooth as a pinkie nail
chanced up out of the waves' reach.

Hold it to light and it changes,
becomes a globe of fractures;
a cavern of ledges and glinting,
not one green but many at once.

And suddenly I think of it bigger
as the whole of the human heart,
carrying the cuts of its journey—
brokenness letting in light.

Gift

Take nothing with you but your shoes.
The path is easy, and once the river opens
into the cupped hands of a pool
swim without fear of being seen.
Walk softly, so sometimes you are surprised
by the full sweetness of birdsong.
The cabin is never locked; anything that's taken
was needed more by someone else.
There is no need of artificial light:
a few candles are enough to warm the dark.
Before you sleep, go out into the silence of the stars
and listen to nothing but the hugeness of the night.

The Small Giant

The otter is ninety percent water
ten percent God.

This is a mastery
we have not fathomed in a million years.

I saw one once, off the teeth of western Scotland,
playing games with the Atlantic—

three feet of gymnastics
taking on an ocean.

The Well

I found a well once
in the dark green heart of a wood

where pigeons ruffled up into a skylight of branches
and disappeared.

The well was old, so mossed and broken
it was almost a part of the wood

gone back to nature. Carefully, almost fearfully,
I looked down into its depths

and saw the lip of water shifting and tilting,
heard the music of dripping stones.

I stretched down, cupped a deep handful
out of the winter darkness of its world

and drank. That water tasted of moss, of secrets,
of ancient meetings, of laughter,

of dark stone, of crystal—
it reached the roots of my being

assuaged a whole summer of thirst.
I have been wandering for that water ever since.

Coll

I remember what it was like to barefoot that house,
wood rooms bleached by light. Days were new voyages, journeys,
coming home a pouring out of stories and of starfish.
The sun never died completely in the night,
the skies just turned luminous, the wind
tugged at the strings in the grass like a hand
in a harp. I did not sleep, too glad to listen by a window
to the sorrow sounds of the birds
as they swept down in skeins, and rose again, celebrating
all that was summer. I did not sleep, the weight of school
behind and before too great to waste a grain of this.
One four in the morning at first larksong I went west over the dunes,
broke down running onto three miles of white shell sand and stood.
A wave curled and silked the shore in a single seamless breath.
I went naked into the water, ran deep into a green
through which I was translucent. I rejoiced
in something I could not name; I celebrated a wonder
too huge to hold. I trailed home, slow and golden,
dried by the sunlight.

Enough

Out of the scurry of the days
a place of late sunlight, and the sky
swimming into blue unclouded;
the trees held in a bonfire of the last sun.

Enough to wait here by the wood's edge
and let the things still hurrying to be done
fall silent, as the first stars
vague the orange of the far-off east.

Pears

I think of that house in early evening
somewhere at the end of summer.

All the doors and windows open
filled with the afterglow of sun

and the whole house heavy with the scent of pears.
There in the lawn that ancient tree

a hundred summers old, and maybe more,
around it a deep, dark ring of pears.

I picked them hour after long hour
to thud into baskets, heavy and melting—

leaving only the broken ones,
all drizzled and wandering with wasps,

and it was as if the house became some strange ship
I was filling for a long voyage

that the rest of our lives might be made of pears.

Salt

When you have forgotten what it means
to have the wind hurrying your window all night long
it's time to find the island. There is a gate—
beyond, a track that's made of sand
winding down the beach. You'll hear the sea
long before you're there, or the shoulders of the island
have opened so that all the horses of the west
are galloping the beach, again and now again.
And if you should open too and let in light,
it is because the breakages within you are so many
and the salt, no matter how it hurts, will heal.

Gliese 581

If we should find some other star—
half a century away, still in the silence of the sky—

we'd leave (the ones who had the money for the fare),
this planet gassed and poisoned by our wars.

We'd look back one last time in wonder
on the blue beauty of our home left empty:

a gust of toppled promises,
growing further off (but never less).

Then dark and doubt, and fifty years
to get to somewhere only telescopes had seen;

unbegun and perfect,
our chance to start again.

And in the beginning we'd believe we could:
we'd keep our promises for sure.

But then the shadow of ourselves
would fall, we would forget—

and on the eighth day we'd be whispering for war.

The Hermit's Cell

I had to listen for a silence
that was born inside.
It took a whole year to find
and now it does not fail.

I need nothing:
all I want is where I am.

I used to pray, and praying then
was struggle with myself.
Now I am made prayer, am hollowed out—
a song that needs no sound.

I pick the blow of flowers, bring them back
in blues and reds and golds,
and in the slow of winter dark
I watch for dawn and know
that I am growing into light
a little every day.

September

The fields lay white beneath a snow of sun
and birds were restless underneath, they rose and wheeled
like silver leaves. The skies were more than blue;
burnished and beaten with a strange brilliance.
The angels are coming, I thought;
the angels will come in the night
when a huge moon ovals through these bright and cloudless skies;
they will come to bind the sheaves
while we are fast asleep.
They will work the fields, their wings tight-folded,
all through the white night of this September,
the moon gliding high like a balloon
over the glazed harvest of the world;
nothing moving except the angels and the wind, until the task is done
in the warm stillness of the dawn.

The Beehive Cells

What drove their feet to these scree islands
scarcely more than whalebacks in the sea,
to build shale haystacks under one huge grey wind,
to spend their dust of years huddled in the keen
of sleet and rain on islands gnawed to knucklebones
of winter gale? Nothing but this flint of faith
that lit a single flickering of lamp, and the sun
that after dark burst big and orange, beautiful
through morning, sometimes, to everything the heart.

Together

Something about going together
out into the night, through stillness—
a darkness mothed with quiet.
And how she takes his hand in hers
and points to a sky all breathed with stars,
and there the first one falling in a silver streak.
Her eyes come back to him and he remembers
how they have journeyed through the winters
to find this place of safety now at last.

He looks with her and sees the stars
come falling over one another down into their night
so soft and silent, beautiful bright trails;
some scratches on the sky, some strokes of chalk.
He holds the warmth of her, that hand
with which she's held his life together
and asks that they might know
a path that's somehow just the same
of beauty and of light.

Autumn

I opened the door into the wood and listened:
through the low wool of the mist
the last leaves dwindled like dancers
down to a golden floor.

It was me that broke the silence:
my boots splintered a single twig
so the whole wood shook and rattled with wings;
the roe deer froze, their eyes all glazed.

Everything listened then—
the silence a waiting, the quiet a watching;
until my feet had disappeared, my shadow passed,
and only the rain fell still in soft glass beads.

Awakening

Out of twelve acorns I picked in the wood
just one grew tall. I'd been away
the first half of July, came back
to thunder, floods, a garden gone to seed.
And then, that evening, I saw the stem
rising high as my hand.

I bent to behold a miracle, the bitterness
of weeds and grass all gone.
I touched three leaves—crinkled things
with cut-out edges, like those of grown-up oaks.
Eleven acorns still lay fast asleep
deep in dark earth. One had become a tree.

The Fishing

The burn flowed down the hillside
like a tousled collie. We climbed and climbed.
A spit of rain in the air; edges of sky
furred with mist. And there, the loch, at last,
like a gem in the brooch of the moors.

The canvas bag with the rod,
the sizzle of the reel,
the search for the best place to cast.

I chased a blue gust of damselflies
then sat and listened to the silence;
the huge emptiness of the hills
buried under a rubble of cloud.

There was always one fish, slippery,
and the heathery smoke of fire,
till the dark sank and the rain began for good.

I see it now, years back across the moorland,
that what mattered was not the fish at all
but everything else.

A Poem for Ann

Three feet small
with dreams as big as Christmas.

A cornfield of curls
and a smile that would melt a soldier.

When you cry
all of you falls to pieces;
everyone comes running to mend you.

At night your eyes look huge:
you are afraid of the owl
that ghosts your bedroom window.

I tell you a story
but you are kingdoms and princes away
long before the ending.

In the morning I will bring you blackbirds
and put the sun on your pillow.
I will tie your laces
and pray safe roads for your feet.

Hebrides

This shattered place, this place of fragments,
a play of wind and sea and light,
shifting always, becoming and diminishing;
out of nowhere the full brightness of morning
blown away, buried and lost.

And yet, if you have faith, if you wait long enough,
there will be the miracle of an otter
turning water into somersaults;
the jet blackness of a loch brought back to life
by the sudden touch of sun.

But you will take nothing home with you
save your own changedness,
and this wind that will waken you
sometimes, all your life, yearning to return.

Remember

There will be only a few days like this—
the low sun flinting the house
through the green sea of the trees as you stand
struck, blessed, bathed in the same light
that rose life once from the young earth, that appled
the first child's cheeks.
There will be only a few days like this
to stop doing and stand, blinking,
as the leverets tumble in the bright field
and a cuckoo's moss voice calls from a far wood.
Wait until the sun has gone in broken orange
down beneath the hills, and the blue sky
hurts with the sudden shudder of the dusk.
Give thanks and turn and go back home—
for there will be only a few days like this.

Mushrooms

The night before a great moon full of honey
had flowed up behind the hills and poured across the fields.

The leaves were rusting, the wheat whispered
dry and gold in the wind's hands.

Andrew and I went to Foss. We drove over the hills
that were blustery with huge gusts of sunlight.

We stopped and walked to the loch, left two trails
through the grass, came on the mushrooms by accident,

a village of strewn white hats
the folds of their gills underneath as soft as silk.

We almost did not want to take them, as if
it would be theft—wronging the hills, the trees, the grass.

But in the end we did, we picked them with reverence:
and they broke between our hands, we carried them home—

pieces of field, smelling of earth and autumn;
a thanksgiving, a blessing.

The Holy Isle

What was the point of going there
except to be apart, to leave behind
the babble of the voices that could never know
how many angels there were dancing on a pin.
This was beyond: a place where silence spoke—
a few fields scattered in between the rocks,
a well of water for the quenching of their thirst
and beehive cells for shelter come the dark.
These were the simple things that made their lives.
What mattered more was breaking through
from out of solitude and quiet, now and then,
into somewhere else; a realm
where they could know the voice of God,
that took them from the ordinary
into a deeper light and out of time.

The Death of Columba

It was another day. The bell echoed,
a coracle came with news of Ireland
and a fine cut of meat. The sea
wrapped round the island like a mantle of silk.

Everything he did as always, just a beat slower.
They saw nothing; the talk was generous,
the laughter easy; as a lark spun songs
somewhere out of sky that still morning.

Yet the horse came. In the middle of it all,
and the faces turned like full moons;
as that long head rested on his shoulder
and the nostrils, full of hay, flared.

For the horse had heard
dark in the drumbeat of his heart
that edge of death, and wept
softly against the old man's head.

Salt tears like the water that had brought him once
out of the heart of Ireland,
that would take him now
over a last sea, into the land he had lived.

The Heron

The heron is a Presbyterian minister
standing gloomy in his long grey coat
looking at his own reflection in a Sabbath loch.

Every now and again, pronouncing fire and brimstone,
he snatches at an unsuspecting trout
and stands with a lump in his throat.

The congregation of midges laughs at him in Gaelic;
he only prays for them, head bent into grey rain,
as a lark sings psalms half a mile above.

Winter Light

to come through a low blue door
under the high grey roof of a forgotten garden
into a place in winter, roofed by grey sky
the scattered holly berries of a robin's song

nothing is alive yet, all is deep and dark
wintered and fastened, shut into the earth
a book unopened, the whole story of the year
asleep, unwritten, underneath my feet

a door in the low sky opens, sunlight
struggles to silver the ground and fades
soft things of rain whisper and nod and sing—
this is enough, this is all I ask

Remembering the Amish

And I have seen them coming home on summer nights
or bent above the washbowl in the kitchen,
haloed in the window by the low sun's leaving;
soft voices in the fields of gentle men with horses.

And in the town they walk their own way,
as though a reverence for what lies beneath their feet
is in their shoes, and in their eyes a peace
no man may buy and few have ever found.

And sometimes when I meet them I feel like him who went
with all his father's wealth and lived in laughter far away
and woke one day to find he'd nothing left.
I feel like turning just like him for home—

that I may also start again.

Evensong

I open the door and walk;
stone booms and hisses underneath my feet.

The choirboys sing, shrill and beautiful—
a song woven of ancient words,
a Latin crossing to another land,
its loaves and fishes, ochre light.

I do not know the words and yet I sing;
the day is done, light sinks—
my life is open to the sky.

www.ingramcontent.com/pod-product-compliance
Lightning Source LLC
Chambersburg PA
CBHW032053040426
42449CB00007B/1088